Pretty Little Rooms

Pretty Little Rooms

Poems

Katie Chaple

Press 53
Winston-Salem

Press 53
PO Box 30314
Winston-Salem, NC 27130

First Edition

Copyright © 2011 by Katie Chaple

A Tom Lombardo Poetry Selection

All rights reserved, including the right of reproduction in whole or in part in any form. For permission, contact author at editor@Press53.com, or at the address above.

Cover art by Edward Hopper, 1882-1967, *Summer Interior*, 1909.
Oil on canvas, 24 x 29 in. (60.96 x 73.66 cm).
Whitney Museum of American Art, New York;
Josephine N. Hopper Bequest 70.1197.
© Heirs of Josephine N. Hopper,
licensed by the Whitney Museum of American Art.
Photograph by Robert E. Mates

Printed on acid-free paper

ISBN 978-1-935708-39-1

For Travis & Helena
For Daddy, Mama, Eve, Will & Alex

Acknowledgments

Thanks to the editors of the following publications where these poems first appeared, though sometimes in a different form:

32 Poems: "Burying the Fig for Winter"; "31st Birthday, A Partial Death"
Antioch Review: "The Invisible Intruder"
Bellevue Literary Review: "In the British Library Repository"
Birmingham Poetry Review: "Life Is Not a Porno"; "What the Dead Do"
Chattahoochee Review: "Saving Eve"
Crab Orchard Review: "Pretty Little Rooms"
New South: "You and she want to drive all night"
Passages North: "Returning *Madame Bovary*"; "Charlie Chaplin Enters a Charlie Chaplin Look-alike Contest"; "My Epicurean Curse"
Poet Lore: "My Lover Teaches Me Seven Card Stud, Deuces Wild"
Rattle: "Pulling Weeds on Your 30th Birthday"
Southern Humanities Review: "Madame du Barry's Refusal" (winner of the Theodore Christian Hoepfner Award in poetry); "A Drowning"
Southern Poetry Review: "Wayne, Balanced"
Washington Square: "Gross Anatomy"

Thank you to the following for their many kindnesses and generosities: David Bottoms, Chad Davidson, Travis Denton, Stuart Dischell, Gregory Fraser, Thomas Lux, James May, and Chelsea Rathburn.

And a special thanks to Tom Lombardo and Kevin Watson.

Contents

Acknowledgments   vii
Introduction by Tom Lombardo   xi

I.

My Epicurean Curse	3
The Invisible Intruder	4
Returning *Madame Bovary*	5
Nails	6
The Secret Lives of Things	7
Always Pears, Plums, Oranges	8
Life Is Not a Porno	9
My Lover Teachers Me Seven Card Stud, Deuces Wild	11

II.

A Drowning	15
Charlie Chaplin Enters a Charlie Chaplin Look-alike Contest	16
Saving Eve	17
To a Child Not Conceived	18
The Skull of the Comedian	20
The Child Actor	21
Pretty Little Rooms	22

III.

Like Wildfire	25
Reverberation	27
Pulling Weeds on Your 30th Birthday	28
Big Sky	29
Wayne, Balanced	30
You and she want to drive all night	31

IV.

Walking at Night in Orvieto	34
Gatsby Dies	36
Harvesting	37
Madame Du Barry's Refusal	38
In the British Library Repository	41
What the Dead Do	42

V.

Gross Anatomy	45
Monologue of an Assassin	47
Departure	48
Mapping the Heart: A Study	49
The Art of Not Thinking	51
Postcard to You From Home	52
31st Birthday, A Partial Death	53

VI.

And when that engine in the mind starts shuttering	57
Nomenclature	58
Burying the Fig for Winter	59
After Snowfall, Crater Lake	60
The Spider, the Hornet, and the Gods	61
Deluge	64

Introduction
by Tom Lombardo

Like its opening poem, this first collection from Katie Chaple will come at you like an overflowing table of luscious things to consume. What she serves you—an enviable variety of topics—is a fine meal of comestibles, some heavy, some bitter, some tart, and some sweet, but all of them tasty.

Katie Chaple's pretty little rooms are filled with luscious people and scenes that pour forth from her vivid, hyperactive imagination. Each room has its own story. Chaple opens the door to each room for you to take a tantalizing peek, and with her hand on your shoulder, she shoves you in at your first trembling, but you're hooked, room-by-room, titillated by the carnie-like exhibits. She tells each room's story with mesmerizing diction and syntax that drive you forward through startling revelations to phantasmagorical conclusions. Along the way, you meet a variety of characters, both fictional and real, that Chaple uses to propel you from room to room: Nancy Drew solving her cases, Madame du Barry on her way to the guillotine, Charlie Chaplin in a look-alike contest, Gregor Mendel who named so many living things but did not speak, Sylvia Plath, with "a comb of cells, and you,/like the bumblebee queen, alone,/climbed into yours," and Francesco Petrarch, somehow paired with the skull of a woman, whose head took the spot of his own in the sonneteer's tomb, of whom the narrator asks

> Whose body was not loved enough
> that her skull could travel like a pebble,
> could be used to punctuate the line of a man's body?

The people in Chaple's rooms may or may not be well known. A few are archetypes, like the med student, in a bar after working on a cadaver, who tries to pick up girls but instead sees under their skin to their bones and tendons, or the assassin who declares to his victim "you are not anything/but the extension of my arm."

Her rooms expose the essential energy of the lives of 21st Century women. After all, as one poem would lead you to believe, life is not a porno with "cocks like the promise of the road headed West." There are betrayals followed by curses that make you hungry for monkfish. There are roofing nails and punches in the gut that could kill. There are golden anklets of past lovers and poker games that could win you a new gender. Her metaphors and imagery are so incredibly unexpected that you must re-read to make sure.

Her final poem, after she has inundated you with her language, declares:

> Once our language becomes a flood…how do we come to grief?

It's an intriguing question to consider, and coming at the end of this collection, the question nails down what Chaple has accomplished here—she has opened the gates to modern metaphysical questions with a collection that stakes a claim for more to come from this very talented poet.

Tom Lombardo
Poetry Series Editor
Press 53

I.

My Epicurean Curse

I think of what I'd like to leave you with
when I leave: a long oak table
and rather than me splayed out naked across the top—
I'd like to leave you with monkfish
in parchment, covered with slices of mango,
slender green stalks of chives,
the lace of parsley. I'd like to leave you
with opaque glazes, pastries—anything that means
separating eggs, folding in heavy cream, anything
that demands a delicate turn of the wrist. Mousse and meringues
and brioche, and Andalusian partridge wreathed in figs.
Dishes dotted with raspberries, garnished
with mint, crescents of tangerine.

From then on, when you lift a fork or break open a roll,
you'll feel something you should remember,
something familiar, a shape that lurks underneath,
that eludes you momentarily, and swallowing, you return
to this body of food, these heaps and curves
of bowls, platters—and for you,
at a quiet corner table, or hovering over an airplane tray,
or tucked in a padded banquet chair, for you,
monkfish will never be the same.

The Invisible Intruder

I always did want to be Nancy Drew—
think, to be that perfect girl with perfect titian hair,
the perfect powder-blue convertible,
to have two trust-worthy (yet not-quite-as-pretty) friends.
But then, the cute boyfriend, the daddy lawyer
and still to continually, with no true hesitation,
seek out the mysterious, the dangerous?
She did have everything, didn't she? Smart, pretty.
She belonged in the best college, the best sorority,
not skulking in an attic or moss-covered mansion.
I think there is something dark in Drew.
I mean, a girl who, if tied, knows how to clasp her hands together
so she can free them, is a girl who possesses
more than a nodding acquaintance with bondage,
who knows more than she lets on.
But maybe Nancy needed a reckless man,
one with a motorcycle—not that androgynous, blonde Ned,
all chaste pecks and letterman's jacket.
Maybe, though, Nancy really wanted to fill up the abandoned
and decaying, where she would wind up, alone,
again and again—in the caves, the towers,
or maybe, really it was all about her dead mother,
and she was trying to pull the emptiness in—
the swirl of air, dankness—by learning it,
by throwing herself into what, in actuality, terrified her.
But whatever it is, tell me
that a girl who's always using her beautiful, slender fingers
to creak open doors, carry heavy flashlights
all to illuminate cob-webbed corners, abandoned passageways,
tell me she is happy with her life.

Returning *Madame Bovary*

At the bookstore counter, I wait
on a cashier who won't take my return
without managerial approval, to be granted by Bill,
who is on managerial break,
and I wonder what if, what if I lean
across this counter, scattering the blue
and black ink pens, the red-foiled chocolates,
and grab his narrow necktie,
choke him slightly, pull
his pocked face to mine and kiss him,
pushing my tongue into his mouth,
while sliding my hand down the front
of his flat-front khakis,
then would I get what I want?

After all, isn't that what we all want:
to be pursued with single-minded urgency?
To have customers, lovers, readers
like the man sitting in prison
for ten years with only his mother and blonde cousin for visitors?
To have him reach through the bars
to what's past them—
to the female prison guard who lingers,
studies her nails, counts floor tiles,
like she's waiting for something
more than the end of the shift?

Nails

are held in the mouth
of a gun and splinter pines
or stab flashing, metal superior
in its point. They get hit
or pounded to hold up
collector plates or families.
Our house's nails recognize
one another in their sharpness,
know the weight they carry—
they will outlast us,
and the timbers above us,
those little pikes cleaving
one to another as you
sleep on your side,
and I lie awake in our bed
while what is between us
gathers, galvanizes
into something I can strike.

The Secret Lives of Things

I wasn't thinking of adulterous wives
when wondering aloud
at how things get lost and lead hidden lives.
The yellow scarf slides behind the dresser,
the sequined clutch slips inside the charity box,
a thread-thin gold anklet falls into the gutter,
disappears without a nick or nod.

I wasn't conscious of your first wife's lover
while scouring the house, rummaging
underwear drawers, feeling under the bed,
retracing my steps, my memories.
You searched and asked
for every pin, stitch and strap.

Instead, I talked of how I never found
what I was looking for.
I found other things,
things I didn't remember having—
the ice crusher, pink sponge rollers,
that deck of 1940s airplane playing cards.

I wasn't thinking of you at all,
until you said, *It isn't things getting lost,
you're the one who's forgotten.* And then I knew
that what I was looking for
is wedged behind dresser drawers,
or picked out of the dumpster on 8th,
bought at some garage sale in Boise,
or is, by now, found on someone else's ankle.

Always Pears, Plums, Oranges

We have the painters and poets to blame,
those artists' dark still lifes, the halo of fruit surfacing
out of mahogany, the plumpness
of citrus and plum, glowing as though some great child
were within. The poets with pyramids
of grapes, the sun of the orange,
then all those pears—the sliding hourglass
of a man's hands, and, of course, the fall apples.
All in abundance. Then there, in the back, an extra,
like a jar of paperclips, a shadow is the banana—
for the bow of interest, for a little reality. A glimpse
of what isn't rounded, of what isn't easily picked,
doesn't fit effortlessly in the hand. After all, how romantic
is its plunk into cereal? The slick slip of peel.
The red lips closing around the barrel. Easy
jokes: Is that a banana in your pocket? Yes,
we have no bananas. A reminder of what's hard
and unlikely. Where are the bananas?
There—a bunch, the curve
of an open, empty palm.

Life Is Not a Porno

Because nothing would get done. Ever.

Librarians and milkmen and nurses and doctors,
flight attendants, pilots—all just jobs
and breasts, hair and moans.

Cocks like the promise of roads West,
clumsy, inept women with no panties,
women who slip and fall at every turn,
their legs making wild Vs.

Naughty bits accidentally exposed, falling out of poorly
seamstressed clothing—impossibility made possible.
Women with red, glossy lips that sigh and scream,
that never utter, "make the bed" or "you never touch me anymore,"
"take out the trash," "mend the gutter," "walk the dog,"
"please hush, we're in a library."

Little to no excuse needed to shed
our niceties results in our undoing
of years of manners and pleasantries.
No dates or phone calls,
no phone bill or infomercials,
no ice or saran wrap—
or at least none with their everyday uses.

Who could go to the store for milk without coming
across a woman in trenchcoat and stilettos
walking through the produce, budding possibilities
shimmering underneath waterproof material?
And you, in tweed, leather elbows,
approach her—no words needed, not even single-syllabled ones,
no meeting of lips, just untying, unbuttoning, removing,
drawing everything back to the undone.

My Lover Teaches Me Seven Card Stud, Deuces Wild

I should have been a man
with a paunch and receding hairline,
with a gold nugget pinky ring,
a man who can read signs like a lover,
a lover who knows what she means
when his woman, without thinking,
brushes her fingertips across her clavicle.
What would it be like to have a name
like Kamikaze Kid, Devilfish, or Diamond Jack,
a name like the edge of a knife?
Think, to play against the probabilities,
to live by the slick slip of cards—
I could tell the bluffs and hide my own,
see clearly what I couldn't know for sure,
mask my beating insides behind a cigar,
a slug of whiskey. Sitting here across from you,
I don't need your hand pushing my cards
toward my chest, I need the breath,
the kiss of a lady against the back of my neck.

II.

A Drowning

We sit in the club with gin, candlelight, and a magician
performing small acts from table to table.
You run fingers over my wrist as though practicing
some sleight of hand, but you're wondering when we'll fall apart.
Drunk and trying to dispel the moment,
I hold the candle at an angle, so the flame licks glass.
The heat builds, burns my fingers, but I hold it
until the glass pops, cracks. Then I laugh, my trick done.

You tell me about Houdini as a child, almost
drowned in a small lake, instead spending
his life in immersion—time and again, chained,
bound, boxed, lowered into icy water.
I am impressed when you explain the years
spent building a threshold for pain
until he could endure The Chinese Water Torture,
until he could endure The Chinese Water Torture with a broken ankle,
which stung more than the stomachache he'd noticed
before the sucker punch from the college boxer.

He might have felt a chill resting between acts
backstage, but would have chalked it up to water.
Until Detroit, where he had to admit he hurt.
Fever over 105. The doctors convinced him
to let them operate. They opened
The Man Who Defeated Death—
revealed insides already corroding, already flooded.

Charlie Chaplin Enters a Charlie Chaplin Look-alike Contest

And comes in third.

How nice to have confirmed something you already know:
there are two others—but that is only here, in Monte Carlo.
Who knows about other cities: Warsaw, Lima, Darjeeling?
You will never meet all these who better tipple
down the street, whose eyes are larger, mournful.
That these others could grip and project
your fear of the orphanage, dead father,
soprano mother's asylum voice strained to madness
delights you—it is all a joke, these props: the bowler,
bamboo cane, toothbrush mustache.
                                    The judges and crowd laugh
and laugh, some doubling over, and from the wings,
you understand laughter borders tears. How nice to understand
that you are not the most yourself. As you wander through
this funhouse of mirrors, you realize the contestants
aren't in disguise at all, but your selves, each a reel of stories
you film in your head in Technicolor, in jingle and hum, in a plunge
of clatter and echo—all selves moving, pantomiming the pantomime.

Saving Eve
for my sister

Slipped down a slope of mud-covered concrete
toward the James River, you were six. I pulled you back
over the lip to the frosted grass:
the front of your pink coat, your tennis shoes,
slick, twigs and leaves clinging to your hair.
Holding your hand, I walked you back.

Years later, Mother told me to write about it
for a Miss Tempus Fugit questionnaire—
how I'd been eleven, it was cold and how you
would have died had you dropped into the water.
Mother said we had you twice over—
thinking back to when you were a baby with meningitis,
snow falling from the biggest blizzard Atlanta had seen,
and doctors uttering you'd be blind or deaf or dead.

Sometimes when we're at the family table,
and you're laughing across from me,
I can believe it is a small thing
that everyone thinks I rescued you,
but really how it was I that urged you
to step onto that grey lap of water,
and how I wanted to myself, but was afraid,
and that you might not even remember
that bronzed statue of Pocahontas on our way from the river,
her arms out, palms up.

To a Child Not Conceived

I left you with my ex
and my mother's hopes.
My message from here, almost forty
and over-worked, is not of regret,
not for your transparent blondeness,
your miniscule toenails, for why
would you have wanted to grow
into a suburbia where you'd try,
like me, to get the very life
you wanted to leave behind?
You'd want boys you truly didn't,
where monkishness would be better.
You'd fight to expunge, leave
behind the best friend as part of the concrete
road dividers and spaced dogwoods,
storefronts and handbags. Take
a path that does not lead
to amniotic fluid, a slit across the belly,
with an abandoned set of college roommates.
You'd turn to a love affair that you'd turn
to smoke like the forest fires out West,
then return to the childhood
sweetheart husband who one Easter
bound your hands, stuffed your mouth,
who, a child himself, called you *piggy*,
spat *divorce* like a wish.
I'd leave him too,
with dildos for remembrance,
leave the house ablaze

with all lights on, so he could see
how empty it was.
Wouldn't look back.
So why tell you this?
I don't know you.
I am talking to myself,
to my hands.

The Skull of the Comedian

On his deathbed, Del Close is relieved,
I'm tired of being the funniest one in the room.
And now, with broken lines and missed cues,
his skull is revived as Yorick
night after night in Chicago's Goodman Theater,
evidence of not being, a witness to mad players.
Rather than clay, webs and beetles,
the lines swirl through the eye sockets
into a cavern that held a civilization,
abandoned, and now audiences
imagine it held a different one—the poor jester.
Held up as a cautionary tale, a vision here,
where the joke lies, at the center, still
with the jester—as all the major players
will become, in the end, a version of this fool,
and then the whole plays
again and again for nights running
as the acts, the lines spill,
layer, thick like echoes
rounded from the mouths of versions of versions.

The Child Actor

His life is a series of settings, a prop room
with mechanical sharks that don't feed;
artificial turf studded with palms
flown in from Tonga. All this
he thinks about so much it becomes his memory:
a brass bed, samurai sword, Model T.
Any woman can be his mother—
the redhead or one with severe myopia, or one with huge breasts.
He knows these mothers change like the silk screen
backdrops and that they wobble and weave or sleep
in blindfolds. He knows that life does not occur
chronologically—the end, the midnight chase
through sleeper cars, happens before breakfast; the villain dies
only to be reborn to twirl his mustache; the boy is tucked in
with a black eye before wrestling with a bully on the playground.
His injuries are painted and erased—a crutch, sling or eye patch
thrown aside—the boy made whole again in a dressing room.
His false smiles bring tears from the girlfriends
of heroes and villains alike. His imaginings
have been rubbed out like eyes out of sleep.
Awake, fingering the stars, flying in the atmosphere,
which he knows to be a back-lot soundstage, he believes
that no one else sees the monster
or its strings, and so he will fall toward innocence:
in time, he will drink or snort or jump to discover
that the greatest imagining is found in a math book,
where there is a single answer to trains
rushing toward one another
in the night at different speeds.

Pretty Little Rooms

—The remains of who was thought to be the Renaissance poet Francesco Petrarch are instead those of two different people, DNA tests have confirmed.

The skull was unexpected, a surprise in the pink marble tomb.
In 1873, the old doctor of Padua claimed it had crumbled,
as though too injured to live outside that stone room.
Did he keep it on his desk? On his shelf as a specimen,
an exemplar of perfection, the knitted plates
a symbol of all that we cannot know of love?

The doctor was not the only man who needed—a friar fled
his flagged cell, hacked off the poet's arm, spirited it back,
a drunk friar in such grief for the world, so moved
as to steal the physical. And where and how to keep it—
this limb that had once moved to love's measure?

And now, these scientists with their test tubes, their milliliters
and tweezers are used to wounds and hairs, blood
and shatter. In their white coats and labs, they don't ask
questions they don't know the answers to. They brush
away quarry dust, measure the circumference, count the alleles,
and approximate the years—all equating female.
Nobody asks: Whose body was not loved enough
that her skull could travel like a pebble,
could be used to punctuate the line of a man's body?

III.

Like Wildfire

I.

When I think of you, I think of you
lifting your hand, calling across the restaurant
surprised to find me again, years later,
in a distant city at the onset of fall,
the trees already turned.
That we met again once you were married
I can believe was accident.

Despite your corner herb garden, her bone china,
the balance of bedside tables,
we drank gimlets at the back of a bar
where Asian women danced, their sequined gowns
warbling light across our table. Drunk,
you pointed, *They remind me of feathers.*
In the motel parking lot, we sat in your car
street lamps strung in the fog
like the bar's votives, haloed, pulsing.
You asked me to drive
all night for Cuban flat bread.

II.
Last time you left, started over
with your wife in New Mexico,
your car window down,
heft of trailer hitched to the bumper,
backseat packed with heirloom candlesticks,
goblets nestled in newspaper, cushioned in kitchen towels,
your hair rustled, your blue shirt snapped flat
against your arm as you drove away.

When I think of you, I see wildfires,
the ones you must see above the Rio Grande,
like emergency flares swollen by gusts across a terrain
which, if not for that distant burning,
would only darken against darkness.
That's when I believe I understand
how these things begin—your wave,
the strike of sulfur, the answering flicker of my hand.

Reverberation

Metaphors stick, you insist,
while splashing oil into a sauce pan,
and I wonder if in fifteen years,
when you are beating eggs
or skimming some cookbook's appendix
for substitutions for cream,
you will recall
this conversation about nothing much
in the same way dough sticks to fingers
and rises to fill the dents they leave.

But then you start
proclaiming the merits of *lingering response*
while throwing onions into the oil,
and when you grasp my arm and your fingers
leave white imprints that slip to red,
I think of your bike tire slicing a puddle,
water lapping back, closing
that glimpse of damp asphalt,
and the tire gleaming with the same water,
a fading imprint of darkened lace on the road.

Pulling Weeds on Your 30th Birthday

Today you shouldn't put your hands in the dirt
or be out in early morning. You should be wary
of sentimentality, when thinking of a year ago,
the first dandelion leading to other dandelions,
to gypsyflower clusters—their clumped roots,
worked, pop like buttons. Some roots are like finessing
a rusty zipper, or those that pull
like the innocent tug of a string and the whole
hem unravels. I should have told you
weeding next to camellias never goes well—
every time you get close another petal slips,
sometimes whole blossoms shatter. You forget
to look up, the flowering trees—
each like the breast of a bird in full plume,
nesting. Each the snowy bloom of apology.

Big Sky

Someone drunk suggested a drive to North Dakota
to see the albino buffalo just born,
and now, more than twenty-four hours later,
the boys stand outside a locked gate,
reading *Closed til spring*, wondering
who thought this haul a good idea, contemplating
climbing the fence or crashing the gate
when a man with a beard wanders out of the house by the road,
and with the offering of a bottle of whiskey,
he's convinced to let them drive on through.

When they find the only thing white in the landscape,
which could be a garbage bag, or sheet,
and watch it transform as they drive, they understand
how the rancher could have mistaken it
for something dangerous in early morning,
mistaken it for a coyote—
that would be easier to see than what is there,
a white calf, licked clean by its mother.
They walk as close as they dare
to the newborn, who's still having trouble seeing.

They hope to carry something back,
pick up twigs, pebbles. Light-headed
in the cold, blinking against the brightness,
they commit the calf's white against green
to memory, and something somewhere
inside tries to remember,
that falling forth,
that breathing in and in for the very first time.

Wayne, Balanced

His talent was equilibrium,
tops of pianos, backs of couches, the side of the tub,
and once, even the roofline.
Poised there, two stories closer to the sun,
arms stretched, half a pimento cheese sandwich in one hand,
he ignored his mother's howl
at seeing him so out of reach.
The men shouted upward and a ladder appeared.

The rest of us craned to watch the strange boy,
who at age nine still wouldn't tie his shoes,
walk the peak and lift us now
into a blue that just goes on.
There above the thoughts of trees,
we were almost level with the courthouse clock,
the church spire. If we looked down,
we'd see hands cupped over brows,
open mouths and fathers climbing to pluck us down.

You and she want to drive all night

as though it were like flipping
through a catalogue, picking
the perfect galvanized tub or gardening gloves
or backdoor mat. Your bodies, side by side,
pitch together down some dark patch,
radio light greening your fingers
as you tune to the next song singing
you along highway, the soft peach
of luck hanging before you. You turn foreign
in the dark like syllables, strange and disjointed, but translated
as the seeds of fields transform to towns, then back
into land looking like fathoms
in a soft hour. Shocks and struts
buoyant, you are both vigilant to each curl
of the road. All squeaks with possibility.
You will both decide where to land—no
destination, but a hope to be lost
and found in the same breath. Coiling the night
in, orchards bloom as you approach
sunrise, and you heap your senses—your faces flaming,
your eyes burn. And your hearts?
                                        Your hearts, open mouths.

IV.

Walking at Night in Orvieto

What was it about the silence of the phone
that crawled into me, drove me out
to a church high in an Italian hill town,
then to a bar, to notice the bartender's walk,
pelvis forward, the aggression
of the velvet paintings, red with ghosts
like the silence which may or may not
still exist, but drove me anyway.
The man across the ocean, whose call I waited for
was on his phone most likely
not talking to his dead mother.

And when I left the bar, tilting the streets,
I watched for the man who wore
a shirt the color of poppies sprouting
on the necropoli below, the man
with a lisp who asked, the day I arrived,
Are you German or Californian?
At night, his glasses rendered his eyes street lamps.
He'd appeared on corners and piazzas for days,
once when I'd bought an umbrella,
once with another woman, both following
me to the apothecary, another time in a side street,
pretending to talk on the phone as he watched me,
yet there I was on the night walk,
and the silence of my room followed.

He'd told me of the small church and the Etruscan tombs—
what else could he have wanted? I knew of the olive groves,
caves and art of dead men, knew the streets
by then, had a path down
from the town past the necropoli.

I was afraid, but that night lonely,
so much so I went out looking
for him. Nothing like the dark
to send anyone careening into the dark.
And I thought of that bartender that I could have fucked,
wanted to fuck, but didn't,
so convinced was I that the phone
would never ring again. But I kept walking,
took the path past that church, down to the tombs.
Funny that man in the melon shirt who followed me
never followed me there, even the morning I was all alone,
stepping down into tombs, vacant except for the grass
growing inside them. The wasps swarmed, ready
for sacrifice, but not me, not that day. Those tombs,
I realized, are carved out of me. Loneliness inside
the loneliness of a field—even the dead amputated
from their graves, which I know were laid out
in the grid of their neighborhoods. The poppies
bright on their roofs, I ate an apricot
and an apple from the ground. The fruit,
which ripens season after season,
with the dead not there to eat it.

Gatsby Dies

Above the moon is an egg, glowing,
a moon that will not hatch, but will shine like a coin
but not multiply, will merely give way to heat,
which will cause fan and white and curl.

Below, the spinning continues—glimmer of spangle,
trumpet, glass, ice, and the pool and the lake
ripple to the moon and away from the light—
faintly, faintly.

What are the rest of us to track?
No boat-shoed low brow in pursuit
of the not-so-innocent innocent,
that something worse than a slut,
a woman hinged on the moon.

So, if you're the wrong man
don't fall in love with the right woman.
But even so, for you, that love leads only to the moneylender,
glasses of wheat, a dark curve that straightens.
Don't gild the flesh. You have no convenient
swimming pool to die in.

Harvesting

On TV, the starlet starved into madness
dove into black air; the B-movie actress
last seen in a red sedan,
driving off with some blonde dame
and a slick-haired guy with grey felt hat, is swallowed
by the dark humidity; the leading lady
crushing valium into her Manhattans
slips and sinks into water.

Skittish sirens, I want your children, the survivors.
Not the young ones, graveside,
staring at adult knees, sky and dirt,
but them later, once they resurface.
Once I can find the lines of their mothers
in a tilt or shape, and I can see
what has happened emerge in their skin,
when they become like Ama pearlers
who slice through waves,
push toward the bottom,
recognize the pressure
on their bodies, make a tight knot
at center, and harvest the oysters,
turn, plant their feet in silt,
and push once again toward the air, survivors
who rise, bodies streaming, hands filled with shells.

Madame Du Barry's Refusal

> *Men of limited intelligence lack the imagination*
> *to be touched by inner suffering, and the populace*
> *is more easily stirred by pity than by admiration.*
>   —Elisabeth Vigée-Lebrun
>   on Madame Jeanne Du Barry's execution

I.
September, 1761

Monsieur Duval,
Yes, I have told you, and repeat it: I love you dearly.
If I did not love you, I would try to get money from you;
I would say, you shall begin by renting a room
and furnishing it, but as you told me that you are not rich,
you can take me to your own place.
It will not cost you anymore in rent, nor more for your table
and the rest of your housekeeping. To keep me
and my headdress will be the only expense—
and for those
give me one hundred livres a month,
and that will include everything.
Thus we could both live happily, and you would never again
have to complain about my refusal.

I begin to know the world.
I will tell you what I suggest, now: pay attention.
I don't want to remain a shopgirl, but a little more my own mistress,
and would therefore like to find someone to keep me.
If you love me, accept this proposal;
but if you do not love me, then let each of us try his luck elsewhere.

Good-by, I embrace you heartily.
Jeanne

II.
May, 1770

She wakes, tired of warmth and blue skies.
When she tells him, Louis laughs,
My lady would prefer the winter?
How can I refuse?
Certainly, the King of France can produce snow—
even in spring.

In three hours, thirty footmen have coated
the paths and grasses of the Queen's Grove
with sacks and sacks of refined sugar.

Two liveried footmen pull the sleigh,
with Madame Du Barry, delighted, kicking and squealing.
She lifts her hand to Louis and the court gentlemen
watching from their carriages and horses.
The principal mistress and her entourage
sport ermine muffs, only for play—
they need no coats.
Giggling, they dance in kid boots,
their long gowns catching the sparkle
of snow that will not melt except on their tongues.
Madame drops pinches of sugar into her mouth,
then, sucking in her cheeks,
the sweet syrup slides down her throat.

III.
December, 1793

She had returned from England,
where she'd pawned her jewels, to stay
in her chateau, the one named for her,
given to her by the King.
Yet, they'd come to arrest her, even there.

Outside the prison, the snow had fallen all night long
and was still falling
as the cart approached the crowd.
A voice jeered, *A bit cold out—give the slut
a coat so she doesn't catch her death.*
The people laughed, climbed on top of one another
to see whose head they were clambering for.
As soon as Madame saw the guillotine
with the night's icicles collected at the top
she did something no one else had done,
she shrieked, leaned out to the rags, and begged.

Kicking and screaming,
her arms tied behind her,
they hauled her from the cart to the scaffold.
Her screams drifted out,
shushing the crowd.
And when Sanson finally drove her to her knees,
No, no, it can't be. You're not going to let me die,
looking up into the snow,
as though her voice might melt it as it fell.

In the British Library Repository

I am the one in the mask
because of dust allergies particularly
sensitive to centuries' old documents,
and, when I look, I see our reflections
in the gloss of the table with the buds
of light from the hanging lamps above us.
We each have a box of old letters from a back room—
their folds stiff and the paper the weight of cheesecloth.
I am reading a letter from a shopkeeper in London
to his business partner. It is the same as countless others.
"Business is good," he says, "many customers
though no new shipments to place just yet."
Family, fine—"Beatrice is to marry soon, a butcher
who makes a good living." I scribble a few notes—
though have found nothing.

The other man holds the letters
to his nose, inhaling deeply.
One letter after another, he lifts and smells,
making two piles. He doesn't read or even unfold them,
and my eyes water just to watch.
He is tracing the plague through England
by smell—stricken households sprinkled correspondence
attempting to prevent the spread of the disease.

I turn back to my piles of letters and notes,
remove my mask, lift the letter from my merchant
of silks and ribbons, and detect a faint stench.
I ask. He says, *Vinegar.*

What the Dead Do

All this business about the dead
dancing or drinking or bowling,
maybe moving to Poughkeepsie,
how they envy us or hate or pine,
that they still enjoy
a good game of Scrabble or Parcheesi
is all nonsense.

And if they move at night for you,
rattling the china, rapping walls, creaking
the foundation—they aren't doing it.
If you see them flicker in the mirror,
or as fog in doorways—
it still isn't them. We want to fool around
in cemeteries to make the dead
palpable like a bank of snow.
We try to evoke them with chant,
want them to nudge lamps, finger
our necks even as dread creeps up.

The dead don't do anything
in that immense stretch of quiet
but molder, rot. A few shrivel
in linen or remain suspended
in ice or bog, the important ones
encased behind glass like heirloom vases.

After all, it's not the dead you should fear,
they are only mannequins we bully about
in that long expanse
where our imaginations are wasted.

V.

Gross Anatomy

My cousin tells me about his cadaver, Baby,
as we pass the lab where she lies.
Says that by the second session, he was stripping
the husk of skin, slitting Baby's chest,
cracking the ribs, flipping them open
like the lapels of a vest, to expose that network,
a skein of threads weaving muscles.
He tells me about the mass of wires,
that you tell an artery from a vein by the snap
of it breaking in two like a hair.

The week they work on Baby's head,
his study group goes for gin fizzes on the river front,
a bar with scarred stools and tattooed necks,
straight bones of pool cues and sharp glint of belt buckles.
He's checking out this girl—
her soft slope from neck to collarbone—
and is thinking about how to strike up talk,
how to work in that he is a med student,
when he has a vision of himself
lifting off Baby's face like the lid of a box,
seeing the fullness of eyes. Then, stark white—
the mandible, a bone that cleans up so nicely—
against red cheek muscles.
He sees the loops of tendons bridging
wider, then narrowing to the next bone.

Shaking his head, he sees under everyone's face,
everyone's the same—bartender, couple kissing in the corner,
hanging on, touching each other only with their mouths,
the man with his hand in his pocket, who's been eyeing
the door all night. He knows that it only takes a drag of the knife
to uncover the whole bar. That couple.
He remembers pinching her chin,
pressing closed the gap
between jaws, teeth to bone.

Monologue of an Assassin

Like a declaration of love not returned—
imagine that, and it is possible.
It must be betrayal—then I,
in turn, betray the flesh—
see how cyclical?
And the process is a kind of love, really.
Think of the pulse, a grappling thing you grasp,
and it could be caress. It is all in your hands—
cut of the wire, the bitter cordite,
callus from rope burn.
You close in on the lowest common denominator—
the circumference of a muscle that no longer expands,
contracts. Oh, what capacity—making everything
capable of being cupped in the palm. One could say,
I have a talent for reduction.

And as I step from shadow, I am ancient Greece—
I feel like prophecy,
a fulfilling of contract, I am pulse and lack,
I am the message and the delivery.
You are not a woman in purple walking a dog,
you are not driving your Aerostar to Target,
you are not a quality assurance manager, or waiter.
You are not sound, you are held breath,
you are not wave, or shine,
you are not velvet, you are not,
you are not, you are not anything
but the extension of my arm.

Departure

Take for instance, here, at this cabin above Blue Ridge—
the gravel road, the way it comes together, the three paths,
the way they form a "y"—one leads to us, another
to a dead-end, and the other a route out,
the way the trees look now, in October,
the mountain and how it may mist or not
mist, and you will not know, but it will either mist
or not mist whether you are here to see it or not.
Think of the ex-husband you have not seen for over a year,
that dog you had not seen for over a year
that he had put down while you were here, the friends
who have left before you. Look
at the way the walls sit there, the bed still
and content, with your breath in it or not. The fire
won't start, the stove won't flicker on,
and the sun goes down and comes up, and the rain hits
or doesn't, and though you know what happens,
though you know how it will all go after you go,
and that you would not be surprised,
you know you will miss it
in the way it will not miss you, will not notice
your departure, did not even notice your retriever's death.

Mapping the Heart:
A Study

The problem
            as we've unfolded it
is that one cannot know another's
but only one's own—and maybe not even that—
a point on which we both agree (wholeheartedly),
so let the cardiologist and cartographer confer,
let discipline step in where there is no measure.
Let a methodology be pumped forth.
Show us labs and conventions, bar graphs and percentage;
Powerpoint of mesa and plain, tundra rolling to rainforest;
film of peaks and states, major townships
which bank on tributary, flowing
to delta. Let there be gradations of ruby, red,
maroon,
            salmon trickling to pink—all grades
of elevation and elation.
Participants scribble, eyes squinting for fissures that run
to gorge. There will be definitions. There will be chambers
where fondness dreams and dresses, the strata
where love resides. Levels must shift, tectonic plates
grate and rise. Where lives lust, but here
where the red beam wavers against a diagram,
where the participants, the lecturers, and just-interested parties
trace the arteries of elevators and hallways back
to their colleagues' rooms, follow the floorplan
to broom closets and alleyways.
                        Show them the monitor's jagged lines,

and before the green height and plunge draws flat,
show them the legend, millimeters to miles, the unfolding
that unfolds a rolling expanse.
Oh, let them find the plain that charts
an opening
                where we can all lie down.

The Art of Not Thinking

You count sheep near the woods
of midnight, say those creaks and groans
are nothing. Recite the alphabet backwards,
keep out the scratching that sounds
in the backroom. Let go
of the dark hearth, the chimney housing
its spring nests, its drafts. Close in
on the body—note the weight of limbs,
the taut breasts, ignore the tapping
at the window, the flicker of mirrors. Hold it
at bay, click the tongue, chant Mother Goose.
Hear the owl? Surrender to the grip,
skim the field, crossroads, the fence, but don't land
in the yard. At the well, the unspooling bucket
drops, snaps like the end of the gallows.

Postcard to You From Home

In this back bedroom that goes mostly unused, the light slants as though from that city we visited. In the seesaw-knocks of the dishwasher sounds the back and forth adagio of water. The washer rocks with loads of laundry—its distant noise like the hum and bustle of juke joints. Later, in the dark, the room is a street corner where I watch the sky's trembling weather move from pulsing cadence to fermata, see drunks in doorways, not think of those back home. There are happenings on this corner at night—the streets thump, a woman chases a man down for money. I imagine you in this city.

Imagine it otherwise: The city after hard rain, steam rising, picture windows looking into restaurant kitchens, glamorous girls ready to stream from cafés, meet their lovers, and whatever their flaws (and they are few) can be hidden behind sunglasses, scarves. And there, from across the plaza, cathedral bells again: *maybe, maybe, maybe,* we need to learn is still not *yes*.

31st Birthday, A Partial Death

Again this morning my arms end at the wrists,
hands dead, like static, like the buzz
of television after the end of a broadcast day.
Outside, the shadowed spears
of daffodils and tulips, the bees
      in my hands flex.

I realize today I am older than you will ever be.
I feel I have been creeping forward
to meet you and have turned a moment too late.
You have stopped the spring, the tulips won't bubble
to the surface, the bulbs of the daffodils
won't open, and the oven's golden bulb
      has blown its filament.

Beyond, looking both over my shoulder,
as well as before me, there is your invisible smoke—
oily, heavy, dissipated, but the colony
knows the meaning of smoke—the end
of civilization. I, too, have an oven,
but you faced all the ovens
      on your floor,
           in your building,
                in your city—
a comb of cells, and you,
like the bumblebee queen, alone,
climbed into yours.

VI.

And when that engine in the mind
   starts shuttering,

this, this, this—then you are born, not knowing *now*
starts the beginning of all that will continue
forward and forward, away from what you will call
your earliest memory—sunlight, water, grass,
where a man you love holds you aloft,
your arms, legs free, and you smile at his smile
and reach toward him on the ground,
even while young and still flying.

Nomenclature

Tonight, mother's garden calls *verbena*
past the gate, and dahlias chant *dahlia*, the white spires'
Veronica. Peonies, hollyhocks.
Some have more than one: dianthus,
formerly "pinks," sunflowers once "old maids."
Roses have each their own: Old Blush,
Duchess de Brabrant, Souvenir de la Malmaison.

Then, I fall asleep to chronicles of a 15th-century monk
who took, in French, a vow of silence, cross-pollinated,
bred, and tended his variety—a rose with red
that deepens along the petals, thickens
so that the fringes are black—looking forever
on the edge of rot.
Was there, in his thoughts, a name for it?
One never spoken aloud, a word
like musty wooded places, a prayer in his shaved head, echoing
while hands moved dirt, coaxing seedlings.

Tonight I ride the Amazon
discovering a plant spurred on by moonlight.
It flowers only at night—petals
pouting open, true shade unknown.
Moonlight quiets the pink.
The color slides
down each petal to be swallowed
by the red center, which must end
in that long, slender throat,
and give way to stalk, chlorophyll,
to pale roots grasping at their names.

Burying the Fig for Winter

> *If you tell me that you desire a fig,*
> *I answer you that there must be time.*
> —Epictetus

You dig a grave the shape of a shadow
from the base of the fig tree
to the length of its height.
The fig is your favorite—mysterious,
and because it is ancient,
holding a certain constancy.
You like that there's a story—the wolf
who suckled Romulus and Remus resting under one.

You dig up the tree,
clip roots with the shovel,
tip the fig into the trench.
Covering the trunk, leaves with mulch,
blood branches under your skin.

This mound of dirt will comfort you,
knowing the fig now stretches its light limbs
where wind cannot touch the leaves,
while the world retreats and ground hardens.
You seem far from when the fig blossoms
will grow inside the fruit, concealed in flesh,
when, the sun warming them,
the wasps will crawl into those yellow rooms.

After Snowfall, Crater Lake

Even the plow with its scrubbing engine is quiet,
parting the snow, packing new on old,
to stop the cold. Let it all refreeze
tonight like memory.
The road is cleared for tomorrow;
the lake—dormant volcano—
is clear, and I imagine all
the way to the lake bed. At surface the ripples,
like pendulums, count,
caught in that rhythm.
I think of the tourists,
all the lovers who have ticked
through here—shutter click on shutter click,
held kiss on kiss, word layered on word.

Lake water gentles in a once-fiery volcano,
snow holds the shape of the landscape.
In an upper window of the inn closed for remodeling,
a light flicks on, gold burning through
white, and a figure holds, spreads
arms, encompassing
the scenery, me, everything,
the arms lifted
                and measuring.

The Spider, the Hornet and the Gods

I.
The pregnant hornet
teetered on the spider, pierced
larvae into its head. The spider
        gave in to the hornet's design.
The spider no longer spun
its trap
        but wove back and forth.
        The hornet feasted on its host.
        The spider no longer thought
in circles but in beginnings and ends,
made a bed for the birth.

II.
After a year of meditation, squatting in roots
with no food or drink,
        the boy was Buddha reincarnated.
He carved himself,
became the tree,
        his fingers and limbs stiffened,
        he belonged to the wind.
Men shielded him at night
        from those who wanted to see,
and so be touched, to take mercy
        from that which would not look upon them.
One evening, heat rising,
        he transformed, left
        the statue he made of himself,
        left only clothing behind, a husk for the earthly.
He was missing
        from the jungle of Bara.
        There was a search party.

III.
No rain. The women believed
they could bring it down,
                        coax the sprouts, revive the village.
Naked, they jiggled and writhed, arms up.
They made dust rise
        from their roll and stretch,
                                  their stomp.
The sun saw them and was disturbed
                                  by the beats.
They danced, naked, in the heat.
                Sun beat down, while men
sat in the shade, nodded and grinned,
                saying whether it rained or not was fine by them.

IV.
A man banished
                from the sea in suit and tie,
mouth filled with the foam of notes,
                was found wandering the Isle of Sheppey.
He had no known language, no Slavic tongue,
        no Russian dialect.
The thing left him was the span
        of pinky to thumb,
            the press and release
of pedals like the heart,
                the fingers like horses,
and flats, sharps, adagio, pizzicato.

He cringed from men,
        and his pearl eyes
filled with nothing
but waves of notes,
                brimming with a fantasia

of fugues—
>   all that he played one afternoon
>   at a parish piano
>>   for the group who believed they found him.

He knew only the chronology of creation,
>   the order of notes
>   as they came to him.

He came, it seemed to us,
>   just to resurrect.
>   He was a root, and our teeth hurt.

V.
She stopped to gather the golden apples, ignoring the flesh.
But for losing the race, she gained
the rough, the vulnerable—
marriage. She learned only one thing can be true
at a time, and it was never the one she wished for.

Deluge

Once our language becomes a flood—
the same seep, the rising, followed by rising, the same
inching up walls—when we've not just wrung out our words,
but when the arrangement becomes watermarks on wallpaper—
when we have no new order for words, when the language is blank
as a nighttime body of water,
how do we come to grief?

Would the sadness rain down
in spears of *l*'s or the weaponry of *x*,
line with the rest of the glyphs in phalanxes against us
just when our arsenal of phrase
and sentence is depleted?

And as dusk comes on, how do we speak
the arrow of our pale hero, hair spread,
as his body washes ashore,
floating toward
and away from us?

KATIE CHAPLE has been awarded a Visiting McEver Chair in Poetry from Poetry @ TECH as well as residencies from Bread Loaf and the Vermont Studio Center. She is currently the editor of *Terminus Magazine* and teaches poetry and writing at the University of West Georgia. Her work has been widely published in magazines and journals, such as *Antioch Review*, *Birmingham Poetry Review*, *Crab Orchard Review*, *Passages North*, and *Washington Square*, among others.

www.ingramcontent.com/pod-product-compliance
Lightning Source LLC
Chambersburg PA
CBHW051701040426
42446CB00009B/1251